CONTENTS

INTRODUCTION

This framework to be completed will help you set up an objective analysis routine to find undervalued projects with a lot of potential. You will reduce the risks for your long-term crypto assets investments by doing your own fundamental analysis.

- Assign a rating based on a comparison with the market average (refer to the table below)
- When higher risks are identified, be sure to identify them in red
- The concept is to refine your metrics by comparing them to other projects
- Over time, you will gain experience and there will be more and more competition that will affect the scores initially assigned. This analysis should be reviewed and updated on a quarterly basis.
- The success of the analyzed project is the ultimate arbiter.
- You must monitor the progress of each project analyzed and learn from successes and failures. If a project achieves your objectives, it means that your analysis is excellent, on the other hand, if a project fails, you will have to question the elements you have misidentified.

Fundamental points 1 & 2 must reach more than 60% to continue the analysis.

To take less risk in your investments, favour "unique" projects with a score of more than 80%.

How to fill in the tables ?			
Term	**Description**	**Rating on 5**	**% Total**
Low	Lack of clarity, direction and extreme risk	1	< 20%
Below average	Missing elements compared to the competition	2	40%
In Average	In line with the rest of the market	3	50%
Strong	competitive / market elements	4	70%
Unique	Exceptional or unique proposal	5	>80%

PROJECT NAME

Symbol

CHANGE LOGBOOK	
Date	**Modifications**

BRIEF DESCRIPTION

OVERVIEW	
Symbol	
Sector	
Price	
ICO Price	
Market Cap	
Circulating supply	
Total Supply	
Token type (ex :ERC20)	
Live Product	
Staking / Masternode	
Website	

SUMMARY OF THE KEYS POINTS

#	Theme	Description	%
01	Token Economics		/35
02	Project		/50
03	Team		/30
04	Company		/20
05	Communication		/30
06	Community		/15
07	Risk		/15
		TOTAL	/195

01 – TOKEN ECONOMICS

#	Metric	Description + Risk factors	Note (0-5)
01	Liquidity Token		
02	Market Cap		
03	Circulating supply		
04	Limited token number		
05	Interest in keeping it staking or masternode		
06	Policy applied to increase its value		
07	Presence on the main exchanges		
		TOTAL	/35
			%

02 – PROJECT

#	Metric	Description + Risk factors	Note (0-5)
01	White Paper quality		
02	Clarity of the proposal		
03	Interest		
04	Market and potential growth		
05	Presence and scope of clients		
06	Competition		
07	Roadmap and respect milestones		
08	MVP		
09	Timing		
10	Realistic fundraising		
		TOTAL	/35
			%

03 – TEAM

#	Metric	Description + Risk factors	Note (0-5)
01	Team size		
02	Previous experience in similar positions		
03	Presence of managerial rather than technical profiles		
04	Experience in fund management		
05	No red flag		
06	Advisors		
		TOTAL	/30
			%

04 - COMPANY

#	Metric	Description + Risk factors	Note (0-5)
01	Existing compagny		
02	Transparency		
03	Partnership and support from VC		
04	Economic Model		
	Income		
	Expenses		
	Risks for business continuity		
	Valuation of the company		
		TOTAL	/20
			%

05 – COMMUNICATION

#	Metric	Description + Risk factors	Note (0-5)
01	Presence on social networks		
	Youtube		
	Telegram		
	Facebook		
	Twitter		
	Discord		
02	Press articles		
03	Regular publishing		
04	Participation in events		
05	Interview		
06	Partnership and support from VC		
07	No unnecessary or excessive hype		
		TOTAL	/30
			%

06 - COMMUNITY

#	Metric	Description + Risk factors	Note (0-5)
01	Size of the community		
	Youtube		
	Telegram		
	Facebook		
	Twitter		
	Discord		
02	Activity		
03	Evolution		
		TOTAL	/15
			%

07 – RISK

#	Metric	Description + Risk factors	Note (0-5)
01	Market risk		
02	Single risk		
03	Risk reduction		
		TOTAL	/15
			%

ROADMAP

DATE	Description	Respect

CONCLUSION

GENERAL OPINION

UPSIDE POTENTIAL

LONG-TERM INVESTMENT

CALENDAR

DATE   **EVENT**

....

....

....

....

....

....

....

....

....

....

....

....

....

....

....

....

....

....

....

....

....

PROJECT NAME

**Symbol**

CHANGE LOGBOOK	
Date	**Modifications**

BRIEF DESCRIPTION

OVERVIEW	
Symbol	
Sector	
Price	
ICO Price	
Market Cap	
Circulating supply	
Total Supply	
Token type (ex :ERC20)	
Live Product	
Staking / Masternode	
Website	

SUMMARY OF THE KEYS POINTS

#	Theme	Description	%
01	Token Economics		/35
02	Project		/50
03	Team		/30
04	Company		/20
05	Communication		/30
06	Community		/15
07	Risk		/15
		TOTAL	/195

01 – TOKEN ECONOMICS

#	Metric	Description + Risk factors	Note (0-5)
01	Liquidity Token		
02	Market Cap		
03	Circulating supply		
04	Limited token number		
05	Interest in keeping it staking or masternode		
06	Policy applied to increase its value		
07	Presence on the main exchanges		
		TOTAL	/35
			%

02 – PROJECT

#	Metric	Description + Risk factors	Note (0-5)
01	White Paper quality		
02	Clarity of the proposal		
03	Interest		
04	Market and potential growth		
05	Presence and scope of clients		
06	Competition		
07	Roadmap and respect milestones		
08	MVP		
09	Timing		
10	Realistic fundraising		
		TOTAL	/35
			%

03 – TEAM

#	Metric	Description + Risk factors	Note (0-5)	
01	Team size			
02	Previous experience in similar positions			
03	Presence of managerial rather than technical profiles			
04	Experience in fund management			
05	No red flag			
06	Advisors			
			TOTAL	/30
				%

04 – COMPANY

#	Metric	Description + Risk factors	Note (0-5)
01	Existing compagny		
02	Transparency		
03	Partnership and support from VC		
04	Economic Model		
	Income		
	Expenses		
	Risks for business continuity		
	Valuation of the company		
		TOTAL	/20
			%

05 – COMMUNICATION

#	Metric	Description + Risk factors	Note (0-5)
01	Presence on social networks		
	Youtube		
	Telegram		
	Facebook		
	Twitter		
	Discord		
02	Press articles		
03	Regular publishing		
04	Participation in events		
05	Interview		
06	Partnership and support from VC		
07	No unnecessary or excessive hype		
		TOTAL	/30
			%

06 – COMMUNITY

#	Metric	Description + Risk factors	Note (0-5)
01	Size of the community		
	Youtube		
	Telegram		
	Facebook		
	Twitter		
	Discord		
02	Activity		
03	Evolution		
		TOTAL	/15
			%

07 - RISK

#	Metric	Description + Risk factors	Note (0-5)
01	Market risk		
02	Single risk		
03	Risk reduction		
		TOTAL	/15
			%

ROADMAP

DATE	Description	Respect

CONCLUSION

GENERAL OPINION

UPSIDE POTENTIAL

LONG-TERM INVESTMENT

CALENDAR

DATE   **EVENT**

....
....
....
....
....
....
....
....
....
....
....
....
....
....
....
....
....
....
....
....
....

PROJECT NAME

# #

Symbol

CHANGE LOGBOOK	
Date	**Modifications**

BRIEF DESCRIPTION

OVERVIEW	
Symbol	
Sector	
Price	
ICO Price	
Market Cap	
Circulating supply	
Total Supply	
Token type (ex :ERC20)	
Live Product	
Staking / Masternode	
Website	

SUMMARY OF THE KEYS POINTS

#	Theme	Description	%
01	Token Economics		
			/35
02	Project		
			/50
03	Team		
			/30
04	Company		
			/20
05	Communication		
			/30
06	Community		
			/15
07	Risk		
			/15
		TOTAL	/195

01 – TOKEN ECONOMICS

#	Metric	Description + Risk factors	Note (0-5)
01	Liquidity Token		
02	Market Cap		
03	Circulating supply		
04	Limited token number		
05	Interest in keeping it staking or masternode		
06	Policy applied to increase its value		
07	Presence on the main exchanges		
		TOTAL	/35
			%

02 – PROJECT

#	Metric	Description + Risk factors	Note (0-5)
01	White Paper quality		
02	Clarity of the proposal		
03	Interest		
04	Market and potential growth		
05	Presence and scope of clients		
06	Competition		
07	Roadmap and respect milestones		
08	MVP		
09	Timing		
10	Realistic fundraising		
		TOTAL	/35
			%

03 – TEAM

#	Metric	Description + Risk factors	Note (0-5)
01	Team size		
02	Previous experience in similar positions		
03	Presence of managerial rather than technical profiles		
04	Experience in fund management		
05	No red flag		
06	Advisors		
		TOTAL	/30
			%

04 – COMPANY

#	Metric	Description + Risk factors	Note (0-5)
01	Existing compagny		
02	Transparency		
03	Partnership and support from VC		
04	Economic Model		
	Income		
	Expenses		
	Risks for business continuity		
	Valuation of the company		
		TOTAL	/20
			%

05 – COMMUNICATION

#	Metric	Description + Risk factors	Note (0-5)
01	Presence on social networks		
	Youtube		
	Telegram		
	Facebook		
	Twitter		
	Discord		
02	Press articles		
03	Regular publishing		
04	Participation in events		
05	Interview		
06	Partnership and support from VC		
07	No unnecessary or excessive hype		
		TOTAL	/30
			%

06 – COMMUNITY

#	Metric	Description + Risk factors	Note (0-5)
01	Size of the community		
	Youtube		
	Telegram		
	Facebook		
	Twitter		
	Discord		
02	Activity		
03	Evolution		
		TOTAL	/15
			%

07 – RISK

#	Metric	Description + Risk factors	Note (0-5)
01	Market risk		
02	Single risk		
03	Risk reduction		
		TOTAL	/15
			%

ROADMAP

DATE	Description	Respect

CONCLUSION

GENERAL OPINION

UPSIDE POTENTIAL

LONG-TERM INVESTMENT

CALENDAR

DATE   **EVENT**

....
....
....
....
....
....
....
....
....
....
....
....
....
....
....
....
....
....
....
....
....
....
....

PROJECT NAME

Symbol

CHANGE LOGBOOK	
Date	**Modifications**

BRIEF DESCRIPTION

OVERVIEW	
Symbol	
Sector	
Price	
ICO Price	
Market Cap	
Circulating supply	
Total Supply	
Token type (ex :ERC20)	
Live Product	
Staking / Masternode	
Website	

SUMMARY OF THE KEYS POINTS

#	Theme	Description	%
01	Token Economics		/35
02	Project		/50
03	Team		/30
04	Company		/20
05	Communication		/30
06	Community		/15
07	Risk		/15
		TOTAL	/195

01 - TOKEN ECONOMICS

#	Metric	Description + Risk factors	Note (0-5)
01	Liquidity Token		
02	Market Cap		
03	Circulating supply		
04	Limited token number		
05	Interest in keeping it staking or masternode		
06	Policy applied to increase its value		
07	Presence on the main exchanges		
		TOTAL	/35
			%

02 – PROJECT

#	Metric	Description + Risk factors	Note (0-5)
01	White Paper quality		
02	Clarity of the proposal		
03	Interest		
04	Market and potential growth		
05	Presence and scope of clients		
06	Competition		
07	Roadmap and respect milestones		
08	MVP		
09	Timing		
10	Realistic fundraising		
		TOTAL	/35
			%

03 – TEAM

#	Metric	Description + Risk factors	Note (0-5)
01	Team size		
02	Previous experience in similar positions		
03	Presence of managerial rather than technical profiles		
04	Experience in fund management		
05	No red flag		
06	Advisors		
		TOTAL	/30
			%

04 – COMPANY

#	Metric	Description + Risk factors	Note (0-5)
01	Existing compagny		
02	Transparency		
03	Partnership and support from VC		
04	Economic Model		
	Income		
	Expenses		
	Risks for business continuity		
	Valuation of the company		
		TOTAL	/20
			%

05 – COMMUNICATION

#	Metric	Description + Risk factors	Note (0-5)	
01	Presence on social networks			
	Youtube			
	Telegram			
	Facebook			
	Twitter			
	Discord			
02	Press articles			
03	Regular publishing			
04	Participation in events			
05	Interview			
06	Partnership and support from VC			
07	No unnecessary or excessive hype			
			TOTAL	/30
				%

06 - COMMUNITY

#	Metric	Description + Risk factors	Note (0-5)
01	Size of the community		
	Youtube		
	Telegram		
	Facebook		
	Twitter		
	Discord		
02	Activity		
03	Evolution		
		TOTAL	/15
			%

07 – RISK

#	Metric	Description + Risk factors	Note (0-5)
01	Market risk		
02	Single risk		
03	Risk reduction		
		TOTAL	/15
			%

ROADMAP

DATE	Description	Respect

CONCLUSION

GENERAL OPINION

UPSIDE POTENTIAL

LONG-TERM INVESTMENT

CALENDAR

DATE   EVENT

....

....

....

....

....

....

....

....

....

....

....

....

....

....

....

....

....

....

....

....

....

PROJECT NAME

#

Symbol

CHANGE LOGBOOK	
Date	**Modifications**

BRIEF DESCRIPTION

OVERVIEW	
Symbol	
Sector	
Price	
ICO Price	
Market Cap	
Circulating supply	
Total Supply	
Token type (ex :ERC20)	
Live Product	
Staking / Masternode	
Website	

SUMMARY OF THE KEYS POINTS

#	Theme	Description	%
01	Token Economics		/35
02	Project		/50
03	Team		/30
04	Company		/20
05	Communication		/30
06	Community		/15
07	Risk		/15
		TOTAL	/195

01 – TOKEN ECONOMICS

#	Metric	Description + Risk factors	Note (0-5)
01	Liquidity Token		
02	Market Cap		
03	Circulating supply		
04	Limited token number		
05	Interest in keeping it staking or masternode		
06	Policy applied to increase its value		
07	Presence on the main exchanges		
		TOTAL	/35
			%

02 – PROJECT

#	Metric	Description + Risk factors	Note (0-5)
01	White Paper quality		
02	Clarity of the proposal		
03	Interest		
04	Market and potential growth		
05	Presence and scope of clients		
06	Competition		
07	Roadmap and respect milestones		
08	MVP		
09	Timing		
10	Realistic fundraising		
		TOTAL	/35
			%

03 – TEAM

#	Metric	Description + Risk factors	Note (0-5)
01	Team size		
02	Previous experience in similar positions		
03	Presence of managerial rather than technical profiles		
04	Experience in fund management		
05	No red flag		
06	Advisors		
		TOTAL	/30
			%

04 – COMPANY

#	Metric	Description + Risk factors	Note (0-5)
01	Existing compagny		
02	Transparency		
03	Partnership and support from VC		
04	Economic Model		
	Income		
	Expenses		
	Risks for business continuity		
	Valuation of the company		
		TOTAL	/20
			%

05 – COMMUNICATION

#	Metric	Description + Risk factors	Note (0-5)
01	Presence on social networks		
	Youtube		
	Telegram		
	Facebook		
	Twitter		
	Discord		
02	Press articles		
03	Regular publishing		
04	Participation in events		
05	Interview		
06	Partnership and support from VC		
07	No unnecessary or excessive hype		
		TOTAL	/30
			%

06 – COMMUNITY

#	Metric	Description + Risk factors	Note (0-5)	
01	Size of the community			
	Youtube			
	Telegram			
	Facebook			
	Twitter			
	Discord			
02	Activity			
03	Evolution			
			TOTAL	/15
				%

07 - RISK

#	Metric	Description + Risk factors	Note (0-5)
01	Market risk		
02	Single risk		
03	Risk reduction		
		TOTAL	/15
			%

ROADMAP

DATE	Description	Respect

CONCLUSION

GENERAL OPINION

UPSIDE POTENTIAL

LONG-TERM INVESTMENT

CALENDAR

DATE   **EVENT**

....

....

....

....

....

....

....

....

....

....

....

....

....

....

....

....

....

....

....

....

....

PROJECT NAME

#

Symbol

CHANGE LOGBOOK	
Date	**Modifications**

BRIEF DESCRIPTION

OVERVIEW	
Symbol	
Sector	
Price	
ICO Price	
Market Cap	
Circulating supply	
Total Supply	
Token type (ex :ERC20)	
Live Product	
Staking / Masternode	
Website	

SUMMARY OF THE KEYS POINTS

#	Theme	Description	%
01	Token Economics		/35
02	Project		/50
03	Team		/30
04	Company		/20
05	Communication		/30
06	Community		/15
07	Risk		/15
		TOTAL	/195

01 – TOKEN ECONOMICS

#	Metric	Description + Risk factors	Note (0-5)
01	Liquidity Token		
02	Market Cap		
03	Circulating supply		
04	Limited token number		
05	Interest in keeping it staking or masternode		
06	Policy applied to increase its value		
07	Presence on the main exchanges		
		TOTAL	/35
			%

02 - PROJECT

#	Metric	Description + Risk factors	Note (0-5)
01	White Paper quality		
02	Clarity of the proposal		
03	Interest		
04	Market and potential growth		
05	Presence and scope of clients		
06	Competition		
07	Roadmap and respect milestones		
08	MVP		
09	Timing		
10	Realistic fundraising		
		TOTAL	/35
			%

03 – TEAM

#	Metric	Description + Risk factors	Note (0-5)
01	Team size		
02	Previous experience in similar positions		
03	Presence of managerial rather than technical profiles		
04	Experience in fund management		
05	No red flag		
06	Advisors		
		TOTAL	/30
			%

04 – COMPANY

#	Metric	Description + Risk factors	Note (0-5)
01	Existing compagny		
02	Transparency		
03	Partnership and support from VC		
04	Economic Model		
	Income		
	Expenses		
	Risks for business continuity		
	Valuation of the company		
		TOTAL	/20
			%

05 – COMMUNICATION

#	Metric	Description + Risk factors	Note (0-5)
01	Presence on social networks		
	Youtube		
	Telegram		
	Facebook		
	Twitter		
	Discord		
02	Press articles		
03	Regular publishing		
04	Participation in events		
05	Interview		
06	Partnership and support from VC		
07	No unnecessary or excessive hype		
		TOTAL	/30
			%

06 - COMMUNITY

#	Metric	Description + Risk factors	Note (0-5)
01	Size of the community		
	Youtube		
	Telegram		
	Facebook		
	Twitter		
	Discord		
02	Activity		
03	Evolution		
		TOTAL	/15
			%

07 – RISK

#	Metric	Description + Risk factors	Note (0-5)
01	Market risk		
02	Single risk		
03	Risk reduction		
		TOTAL	/15
			%

ROADMAP

DATE	Description	Respect

CONCLUSION

GENERAL OPINION

UPSIDE POTENTIAL

LONG-TERM INVESTMENT

CALENDAR

DATE

EVENT

PROJECT NAME

**Symbol**

CHANGE LOGBOOK	
Date	**Modifications**

BRIEF DESCRIPTION

OVERVIEW	
Symbol	
Sector	
Price	
ICO Price	
Market Cap	
Circulating supply	
Total Supply	
Token type (ex :ERC20)	
Live Product	
Staking / Masternode	
Website	

SUMMARY OF THE KEYS POINTS

#	Theme	Description	%
01	Token Economics		/35
02	Project		/50
03	Team		/30
04	Company		/20
05	Communication		/30
06	Community		/15
07	Risk		/15
		TOTAL	/195

01 – TOKEN ECONOMICS

#	Metric	Description + Risk factors	Note (0-5)
01	Liquidity Token		
02	Market Cap		
03	Circulating supply		
04	Limited token number		
05	Interest in keeping it staking or masternode		
06	Policy applied to increase its value		
07	Presence on the main exchanges		
		TOTAL	/35
			%

02 – PROJECT

#	Metric	Description + Risk factors	Note (0-5)
01	White Paper quality		
02	Clarity of the proposal		
03	Interest		
04	Market and potential growth		
05	Presence and scope of clients		
06	Competition		
07	Roadmap and respect milestones		
08	MVP		
09	Timing		
10	Realistic fundraising		
		TOTAL	/35
			%

03 – TEAM

#	Metric	Description + Risk factors	Note (0-5)
01	Team size		
02	Previous experience in similar positions		
03	Presence of managerial rather than technical profiles		
04	Experience in fund management		
05	No red flag		
06	Advisors		
		TOTAL	/30
			%

04 - COMPANY

#	Metric	Description + Risk factors	Note (0-5)
01	Existing compagny		
02	Transparency		
03	Partnership and support from VC		
04	Economic Model		
	Income		
	Expenses		
	Risks for business continuity		
	Valuation of the company		
		TOTAL	/20
			%

05 – COMMUNICATION

#	Metric	Description + Risk factors	Note (0-5)
01	Presence on social networks		
	Youtube		
	Telegram		
	Facebook		
	Twitter		
	Discord		
02	Press articles		
03	Regular publishing		
04	Participation in events		
05	Interview		
06	Partnership and support from VC		
07	No unnecessary or excessive hype		
		TOTAL	/30
			%

06 - COMMUNITY

#	Metric	Description + Risk factors	Note (0-5)
01	Size of the community		
	Youtube		
	Telegram		
	Facebook		
	Twitter		
	Discord		
02	Activity		
03	Evolution		
		TOTAL	/15
			%

07 – RISK

#	Metric	Description + Risk factors	Note (0-5)
01	Market risk		
02	Single risk		
03	Risk reduction		
		TOTAL	/15
			%

ROADMAP

DATE	Description	Respect

CONCLUSION

GENERAL OPINION

UPSIDE POTENTIAL

LONG-TERM INVESTMENT

CALENDAR

DATE   **EVENT**

....

....

....

....

....

....

....

....

....

....

....

....

....

....

....

....

....

....

....

....

....

....

PROJECT NAME

Symbol

CHANGE LOGBOOK	
Date	**Modifications**

BRIEF DESCRIPTION

OVERVIEW	
Symbol	
Sector	
Price	
ICO Price	
Market Cap	
Circulating supply	
Total Supply	
Token type (ex :ERC20)	
Live Product	
Staking / Masternode	
Website	

SUMMARY OF THE KEYS POINTS

#	Theme	Description	%
01	Token Economics		/35
02	Project		/50
03	Team		/30
04	Company		/20
05	Communication		/30
06	Community		/15
07	Risk		/15
		TOTAL	/195

01 – TOKEN ECONOMICS

#	Metric	Description + Risk factors	Note (0-5)
01	Liquidity Token		
02	Market Cap		
03	Circulating supply		
04	Limited token number		
05	Interest in keeping it staking or masternode		
06	Policy applied to increase its value		
07	Presence on the main exchanges		
		TOTAL	/35
			%

02 – PROJECT

#	Metric	Description + Risk factors	Note (0-5)
01	White Paper quality		
02	Clarity of the proposal		
03	Interest		
04	Market and potential growth		
05	Presence and scope of clients		
06	Competition		
07	Roadmap and respect milestones		
08	MVP		
09	Timing		
10	Realistic fundraising		
		TOTAL	/35
			%

03 - TEAM

#	Metric	Description + Risk factors	Note (0-5)
01	Team size		
02	Previous experience in similar positions		
03	Presence of managerial rather than technical profiles		
04	Experience in fund management		
05	No red flag		
06	Advisors		
		TOTAL	/30
			%

04 – COMPANY

#	Metric	Description + Risk factors	Note (0-5)
01	Existing compagny		
02	Transparency		
03	Partnership and support from VC		
04	Economic Model		
	Income		
	Expenses		
	Risks for business continuity		
	Valuation of the company		
		TOTAL	/20
			%

05 – COMMUNICATION

#	Metric	Description + Risk factors	Note (0-5)
01	Presence on social networks		
	Youtube		
	Telegram		
	Facebook		
	Twitter		
	Discord		
02	Press articles		
03	Regular publishing		
04	Participation in events		
05	Interview		
06	Partnership and support from VC		
07	No unnecessary or excessive hype		
		TOTAL	/30
			%

06 - COMMUNITY

#	Metric	Description + Risk factors	Note (0-5)
01	Size of the community		
	Youtube		
	Telegram		
	Facebook		
	Twitter		
	Discord		
02	Activity		
03	Evolution		
		TOTAL	/15
			%

07 – RISK

#	Metric	Description + Risk factors	Note (0-5)
01	Market risk		
02	Single risk		
03	Risk reduction		
		TOTAL	/15
			%

ROADMAP

DATE	Description	Respect

CONCLUSION

GENERAL OPINION

UPSIDE POTENTIAL

LONG-TERM INVESTMENT

CALENDAR

DATE	EVENT
......	......
......	......
......	......
......	......
......	......
......	......
......	......
......	......
......	......
......	......
......	......
......	......
......	......
......	......
......	......
......	......
......	......
......	......
......	......
......	......
......	......
......	......

PROJECT NAME

Symbol

CHANGE LOGBOOK	
Date	**Modifications**

BRIEF DESCRIPTION

OVERVIEW	
Symbol	
Sector	
Price	
ICO Price	
Market Cap	
Circulating supply	
Total Supply	
Token type (ex :ERC20)	
Live Product	
Staking / Masternode	
Website	

SUMMARY OF THE KEYS POINTS

#	Theme	Description	%
01	Token Economics		/35
02	Project		/50
03	Team		/30
04	Company		/20
05	Communication		/30
06	Community		/15
07	Risk		/15
		TOTAL	/195

01 – TOKEN ECONOMICS

#	Metric	Description + Risk factors	Note (0-5)
01	Liquidity Token		
02	Market Cap		
03	Circulating supply		
04	Limited token number		
05	Interest in keeping it staking or masternode		
06	Policy applied to increase its value		
07	Presence on the main exchanges		
		TOTAL	/35
			%

02 – PROJECT

#	Metric	Description + Risk factors	Note (0-5)
01	White Paper quality		
02	Clarity of the proposal		
03	Interest		
04	Market and potential growth		
05	Presence and scope of clients		
06	Competition		
07	Roadmap and respect milestones		
08	MVP		
09	Timing		
10	Realistic fundraising		
		TOTAL	/35
			%

03 – TEAM

#	Metric	Description + Risk factors	Note (0-5)
01	Team size		
02	Previous experience in similar positions		
03	Presence of managerial rather than technical profiles		
04	Experience in fund management		
05	No red flag		
06	Advisors		
		TOTAL	/30
			%

04 – COMPANY

#	Metric	Description + Risk factors	Note (0-5)
01	Existing compagny		
02	Transparency		
03	Partnership and support from VC		
04	Economic Model		
	Income		
	Expenses		
	Risks for business continuity		
	Valuation of the company		
		TOTAL	/20
			%

05 – COMMUNICATION

#	Metric	Description + Risk factors	Note (0-5)
01	Presence on social networks		
	Youtube		
	Telegram		
	Facebook		
	Twitter		
	Discord		
02	Press articles		
03	Regular publishing		
04	Participation in events		
05	Interview		
06	Partnership and support from VC		
07	No unnecessary or excessive hype		
		TOTAL	/30
			%

06 – COMMUNITY

#	Metric	Description + Risk factors	Note (0-5)
01	Size of the community		
	Youtube		
	Telegram		
	Facebook		
	Twitter		
	Discord		
02	Activity		
03	Evolution		
		TOTAL	/15
			%

07 - RISK

#	Metric	Description + Risk factors	Note (0-5)
01	Market risk		
02	Single risk		
03	Risk reduction		
		TOTAL	/15
			%

ROADMAP

DATE	Description	Respect

CONCLUSION

GENERAL OPINION

UPSIDE POTENTIAL

LONG-TERM INVESTMENT

CALENDAR

DATE	EVENT

PROJECT NAME

#

Symbol

CHANGE LOGBOOK	
Date	**Modifications**

BRIEF DESCRIPTION

OVERVIEW	
Symbol	
Sector	
Price	
ICO Price	
Market Cap	
Circulating supply	
Total Supply	
Token type (ex :ERC20)	
Live Product	
Staking / Masternode	
Website	

SUMMARY OF THE KEYS POINTS

#	Theme	Description	%
01	Token Economics		/35
02	Project		/50
03	Team		/30
04	Company		/20
05	Communication		/30
06	Community		/15
07	Risk		/15
		TOTAL	/195

01 – TOKEN ECONOMICS

#	Metric	Description + Risk factors	Note (0-5)
01	Liquidity Token		
02	Market Cap		
03	Circulating supply		
04	Limited token number		
05	Interest in keeping it staking or masternode		
06	Policy applied to increase its value		
07	Presence on the main exchanges		
		TOTAL	/35
			%

02 – PROJECT

#	Metric	Description + Risk factors	Note (0-5)
01	White Paper quality		
02	Clarity of the proposal		
03	Interest		
04	Market and potential growth		
05	Presence and scope of clients		
06	Competition		
07	Roadmap and respect milestones		
08	MVP		
09	Timing		
10	Realistic fundraising		
		TOTAL	/35
			%

03 – TEAM

#	Metric	Description + Risk factors	Note (0-5)
01	Team size		
02	Previous experience in similar positions		
03	Presence of managerial rather than technical profiles		
04	Experience in fund management		
05	No red flag		
06	Advisors		
		TOTAL	/30
			%

04 – COMPANY

#	Metric	Description + Risk factors	Note (0-5)
01	Existing compagny		
02	Transparency		
03	Partnership and support from VC		
04	Economic Model		
	Income		
	Expenses		
	Risks for business continuity		
	Valuation of the company		
		TOTAL	/20
			%

05 – COMMUNICATION

#	Metric	Description + Risk factors	Note (0-5)
01	Presence on social networks		
	Youtube		
	Telegram		
	Facebook		
	Twitter		
	Discord		
02	Press articles		
03	Regular publishing		
04	Participation in events		
05	Interview		
06	Partnership and support from VC		
07	No unnecessary or excessive hype		
		TOTAL	/30
			%

06 – COMMUNITY

#	Metric	Description + Risk factors	Note (0-5)
01	Size of the community		
	Youtube		
	Telegram		
	Facebook		
	Twitter		
	Discord		
02	Activity		
03	Evolution		
		TOTAL	/15
			%

07 – RISK

#	Metric	Description + Risk factors	Note (0-5)
01	Market risk		
02	Single risk		
03	Risk reduction		
		TOTAL	/15
			%

ROADMAP

DATE	Description	Respect

CONCLUSION

GENERAL OPINION

UPSIDE POTENTIAL

LONG-TERM INVESTMENT

CALENDAR

DATE	EVENT

PROJECT NAME

#

Symbol

CHANGE LOGBOOK	
Date	**Modifications**

BRIEF DESCRIPTION

OVERVIEW	
Symbol	
Sector	
Price	
ICO Price	
Market Cap	
Circulating supply	
Total Supply	
Token type (ex :ERC20)	
Live Product	
Staking / Masternode	
Website	

SUMMARY OF THE KEYS POINTS

#	Theme	Description	%
01	Token Economics		/35
02	Project		/50
03	Team		/30
04	Company		/20
05	Communication		/30
06	Community		/15
07	Risk		/15
		TOTAL	/195

01 – TOKEN ECONOMICS

#	Metric	Description + Risk factors	Note (0-5)
01	Liquidity Token		
02	Market Cap		
03	Circulating supply		
04	Limited token number		
05	Interest in keeping it staking or masternode		
06	Policy applied to increase its value		
07	Presence on the main exchanges		
		TOTAL	/35
			%

02 – PROJECT

#	Metric	Description + Risk factors	Note (0-5)
01	White Paper quality		
02	Clarity of the proposal		
03	Interest		
04	Market and potential growth		
05	Presence and scope of clients		
06	Competition		
07	Roadmap and respect milestones		
08	MVP		
09	Timing		
10	Realistic fundraising		
		TOTAL	/35
			%

03 - TEAM

#	Metric	Description + Risk factors	Note (0-5)
01	Team size		
02	Previous experience in similar positions		
03	Presence of managerial rather than technical profiles		
04	Experience in fund management		
05	No red flag		
06	Advisors		
		TOTAL	/30
			%

04 – COMPANY

#	Metric	Description + Risk factors	Note (0-5)
01	Existing compagny		
02	Transparency		
03	Partnership and support from VC		
04	Economic Model		
	Income		
	Expenses		
	Risks for business continuity		
	Valuation of the company		
		TOTAL	/20
			%

05 – COMMUNICATION

#	Metric	Description + Risk factors	Note (0-5)
01	Presence on social networks		
	Youtube		
	Telegram		
	Facebook		
	Twitter		
	Discord		
02	Press articles		
03	Regular publishing		
04	Participation in events		
05	Interview		
06	Partnership and support from VC		
07	No unnecessary or excessive hype		
		TOTAL	/30
			%

06 – COMMUNITY

#	Metric	Description + Risk factors	Note (0-5)
01	Size of the community		
	Youtube		
	Telegram		
	Facebook		
	Twitter		
	Discord		
02	Activity		
03	Evolution		
		TOTAL	/15
			%

07 – RISK

#	Metric	Description + Risk factors	Note (0-5)
01	Market risk		
02	Single risk		
03	Risk reduction		
		TOTAL	/15
			%

ROADMAP

DATE	Description	Respect

CONCLUSION

GENERAL OPINION

UPSIDE POTENTIAL

LONG-TERM INVESTMENT

CALENDAR

DATE   **EVENT**

....

....

....

....

....

....

....

....

....

....

....

....

....

....

....

....

....

....

....

....

....

....

PROJECT NAME

**Symbol**

CHANGE LOGBOOK	
Date	**Modifications**

BRIEF DESCRIPTION

OVERVIEW	
Symbol	
Sector	
Price	
ICO Price	
Market Cap	
Circulating supply	
Total Supply	
Token type (ex :ERC20)	
Live Product	
Staking / Masternode	
Website	

SUMMARY OF THE KEYS POINTS

#	Theme	Description	%
01	Token Economics		
			/35
02	Project		
			/50
03	Team		
			/30
04	Company		
			/20
05	Communication		
			/30
06	Community		
			/15
07	Risk		
			/15
		TOTAL	/195

01 – TOKEN ECONOMICS

#	Metric	Description + Risk factors	Note (0-5)
01	Liquidity Token		
02	Market Cap		
03	Circulating supply		
04	Limited token number		
05	Interest in keeping it staking or masternode		
06	Policy applied to increase its value		
07	Presence on the main exchanges		
		TOTAL	/35
			%

02 – PROJECT

#	Metric	Description + Risk factors	Note (0-5)
01	White Paper quality		
02	Clarity of the proposal		
03	Interest		
04	Market and potential growth		
05	Presence and scope of clients		
06	Competition		
07	Roadmap and respect milestones		
08	MVP		
09	Timing		
10	Realistic fundraising		
		TOTAL	/35
			%

03 – TEAM

#	Metric	Description + Risk factors	Note (0-5)
01	Team size		
02	Previous experience in similar positions		
03	Presence of managerial rather than technical profiles		
04	Experience in fund management		
05	No red flag		
06	Advisors		
		TOTAL	/30
			%

04 - COMPANY

#	Metric	Description + Risk factors	Note (0-5)
01	Existing compagny		
02	Transparency		
03	Partnership and support from VC		
04	Economic Model		
	Income		
	Expenses		
	Risks for business continuity		
	Valuation of the company		
		TOTAL	/20
			%

05 – COMMUNICATION

#	Metric	Description + Risk factors	Note (0-5)
01	Presence on social networks		
	Youtube		
	Telegram		
	Facebook		
	Twitter		
	Discord		
02	Press articles		
03	Regular publishing		
04	Participation in events		
05	Interview		
06	Partnership and support from VC		
07	No unnecessary or excessive hype		
		TOTAL	/30
			%

06 – COMMUNITY

#	Metric	Description + Risk factors	Note (0-5)
01	Size of the community		
	Youtube		
	Telegram		
	Facebook		
	Twitter		
	Discord		
02	Activity		
03	Evolution		
		TOTAL	/15
			%

07 - RISK

#	Metric	Description + Risk factors	Note (0-5)
01	Market risk		
02	Single risk		
03	Risk reduction		
		TOTAL	/15
			%

ROADMAP

DATE	Description	Respect

CONCLUSION

GENERAL OPINION

UPSIDE POTENTIAL

LONG-TERM INVESTMENT

CALENDAR

DATE   **EVENT**

....

....

....

....

....

....

....

....

....

....

....

....

....

....

....

....

....

....

....

....

....

PROJECT NAME

**Symbol**

CHANGE LOGBOOK	
Date	**Modifications**

BRIEF DESCRIPTION

OVERVIEW	
Symbol	
Sector	
Price	
ICO Price	
Market Cap	
Circulating supply	
Total Supply	
Token type (ex :ERC20)	
Live Product	
Staking / Masternode	
Website	

SUMMARY OF THE KEYS POINTS

#	Theme	Description	%
01	Token Economics		/35
02	Project		/50
03	Team		/30
04	Company		/20
05	Communication		/30
06	Community		/15
07	Risk		/15
		TOTAL	/195

01 - TOKEN ECONOMICS

#	Metric	Description + Risk factors	Note (0-5)
01	Liquidity Token		
02	Market Cap		
03	Circulating supply		
04	Limited token number		
05	Interest in keeping it staking or masternode		
06	Policy applied to increase its value		
07	Presence on the main exchanges		
		TOTAL	/35
			%

02 – PROJECT

#	Metric	Description + Risk factors	Note (0-5)
01	White Paper quality		
02	Clarity of the proposal		
03	Interest		
04	Market and potential growth		
05	Presence and scope of clients		
06	Competition		
07	Roadmap and respect milestones		
08	MVP		
09	Timing		
10	Realistic fundraising		
		TOTAL	/35
			%

03 - TEAM

#	Metric	Description + Risk factors	Note (0-5)
01	Team size		
02	Previous experience in similar positions		
03	Presence of managerial rather than technical profiles		
04	Experience in fund management		
05	No red flag		
06	Advisors		
		TOTAL	/30
			%

04 – COMPANY

#	Metric	Description + Risk factors	Note (0-5)
01	Existing compagny		
02	Transparency		
03	Partnership and support from VC		
04	Economic Model		
	Income		
	Expenses		
	Risks for business continuity		
	Valuation of the company		
		TOTAL	/20
			%

05 – COMMUNICATION

#	Metric	Description + Risk factors	Note (0-5)
01	Presence on social networks		
	Youtube		
	Telegram		
	Facebook		
	Twitter		
	Discord		
02	Press articles		
03	Regular publishing		
04	Participation in events		
05	Interview		
06	Partnership and support from VC		
07	No unnecessary or excessive hype		
		TOTAL	/30
			%

06 – COMMUNITY

#	Metric	Description + Risk factors	Note (0-5)
01	Size of the community		
	Youtube		
	Telegram		
	Facebook		
	Twitter		
	Discord		
02	Activity		
03	Evolution		
		TOTAL	/15
			%

07 – RISK

#	Metric	Description + Risk factors	Note (0-5)
01	Market risk		
02	Single risk		
03	Risk reduction		
		TOTAL	/15
			%

ROADMAP

DATE	Description	Respect

CONCLUSION

GENERAL OPINION

UPSIDE POTENTIAL

LONG-TERM INVESTMENT

CALENDAR

DATE	EVENT

PROJECT NAME

#

Symbol

CHANGE LOGBOOK	
Date	**Modifications**

BRIEF DESCRIPTION

OVERVIEW	
Symbol	
Sector	
Price	
ICO Price	
Market Cap	
Circulating supply	
Total Supply	
Token type (ex :ERC20)	
Live Product	
Staking / Masternode	
Website	

SUMMARY OF THE KEYS POINTS

#	Theme	Description	%
01	Token Economics		/35
02	Project		/50
03	Team		/30
04	Company		/20
05	Communication		/30
06	Community		/15
07	Risk		/15
		TOTAL	/195

01 – TOKEN ECONOMICS

#	Metric	Description + Risk factors	Note (0-5)
01	Liquidity Token		
02	Market Cap		
03	Circulating supply		
04	Limited token number		
05	Interest in keeping it staking or masternode		
06	Policy applied to increase its value		
07	Presence on the main exchanges		
		TOTAL	/35
			%

02 – PROJECT

#	Metric	Description + Risk factors	Note (0-5)
01	White Paper quality		
02	Clarity of the proposal		
03	Interest		
04	Market and potential growth		
05	Presence and scope of clients		
06	Competition		
07	Roadmap and respect milestones		
08	MVP		
09	Timing		
10	Realistic fundraising		
		TOTAL	/35
			%

03 – TEAM

#	Metric	Description + Risk factors	Note (0-5)
01	Team size		
02	Previous experience in similar positions		
03	Presence of managerial rather than technical profiles		
04	Experience in fund management		
05	No red flag		
06	Advisors		
		TOTAL	/30
			%

04 – COMPANY

#	Metric	Description + Risk factors	Note (0-5)
01	Existing compagny		
02	Transparency		
03	Partnership and support from VC		
04	Economic Model		
	Income		
	Expenses		
	Risks for business continuity		
	Valuation of the company		
		TOTAL	/20
			%

05 – COMMUNICATION

#	Metric	Description + Risk factors	Note (0-5)
01	Presence on social networks		
	Youtube		
	Telegram		
	Facebook		
	Twitter		
	Discord		
02	Press articles		
03	Regular publishing		
04	Participation in events		
05	Interview		
06	Partnership and support from VC		
07	No unnecessary or excessive hype		
		TOTAL	/30
			%

06 - COMMUNITY

#	Metric	Description + Risk factors	Note (0-5)
01	Size of the community		
	Youtube		
	Telegram		
	Facebook		
	Twitter		
	Discord		
02	Activity		
03	Evolution		
		TOTAL	/15
			%

07 – RISK

#	Metric	Description + Risk factors	Note (0-5)
01	Market risk		
02	Single risk		
03	Risk reduction		
		TOTAL	/15
			%

ROADMAP

DATE	Description	Respect

CONCLUSION

GENERAL OPINION

UPSIDE POTENTIAL

LONG-TERM INVESTMENT

CALENDAR

DATE	EVENT

PROJECT NAME

#

Symbol

CHANGE LOGBOOK	
Date	**Modifications**

BRIEF DESCRIPTION

OVERVIEW	
Symbol	
Sector	
Price	
ICO Price	
Market Cap	
Circulating supply	
Total Supply	
Token type (ex :ERC20)	
Live Product	
Staking / Masternode	
Website	

SUMMARY OF THE KEYS POINTS

#	Theme	Description	%
01	Token Economics		/35
02	Project		/50
03	Team		/30
04	Company		/20
05	Communication		/30
06	Community		/15
07	Risk		/15
		TOTAL	/195

01 – TOKEN ECONOMICS

#	Metric	Description + Risk factors	Note (0-5)
01	Liquidity Token		
02	Market Cap		
03	Circulating supply		
04	Limited token number		
05	Interest in keeping it staking or masternode		
06	Policy applied to increase its value		
07	Presence on the main exchanges		
		TOTAL	/35
			%

02 – PROJECT

#	Metric	Description + Risk factors	Note (0-5)
01	White Paper quality		
02	Clarity of the proposal		
03	Interest		
04	Market and potential growth		
05	Presence and scope of clients		
06	Competition		
07	Roadmap and respect milestones		
08	MVP		
09	Timing		
10	Realistic fundraising		
		TOTAL	/35
			%

03 – TEAM

#	Metric	Description + Risk factors	Note (0-5)
01	Team size		
02	Previous experience in similar positions		
03	Presence of managerial rather than technical profiles		
04	Experience in fund management		
05	No red flag		
06	Advisors		
		TOTAL	/30
			%

04 - COMPANY

#	Metric	Description + Risk factors	Note (0-5)
01	Existing compagny		
02	Transparency		
03	Partnership and support from VC		
04	Economic Model		
	Income		
	Expenses		
	Risks for business continuity		
	Valuation of the company		
		TOTAL	/20
			%

05 – COMMUNICATION

#	Metric	Description + Risk factors	Note (0-5)
01	Presence on social networks		
	Youtube		
	Telegram		
	Facebook		
	Twitter		
	Discord		
02	Press articles		
03	Regular publishing		
04	Participation in events		
05	Interview		
06	Partnership and support from VC		
07	No unnecessary or excessive hype		
		TOTAL	/30
			%

06 – COMMUNITY

#	Metric	Description + Risk factors	Note (0-5)
01	Size of the community		
	Youtube		
	Telegram		
	Facebook		
	Twitter		
	Discord		
02	Activity		
03	Evolution		
		TOTAL	/15
			%

07 – RISK

#	Metric	Description + Risk factors	Note (0-5)
01	Market risk		
02	Single risk		
03	Risk reduction		
		TOTAL	/15
			%

ROADMAP

DATE	Description	Respect

CONCLUSION

GENERAL OPINION

UPSIDE POTENTIAL

LONG-TERM INVESTMENT

CALENDAR

DATE   **EVENT**

....

....

....

....

....

....

....

....

....

....

....

....

....

....

....

....

....

....

....

....

....

....

PROJECT NAME

#

Symbol

CHANGE LOGBOOK	
Date	**Modifications**

BRIEF DESCRIPTION

OVERVIEW	
Symbol	
Sector	
Price	
ICO Price	
Market Cap	
Circulating supply	
Total Supply	
Token type (ex :ERC20)	
Live Product	
Staking / Masternode	
Website	

SUMMARY OF THE KEYS POINTS

#	Theme	Description	%
01	Token Economics		/35
02	Project		/50
03	Team		/30
04	Company		/20
05	Communication		/30
06	Community		/15
07	Risk		/15
		TOTAL	/195

01 – TOKEN ECONOMICS

#	Metric	Description + Risk factors	Note (0-5)
01	Liquidity Token		
02	Market Cap		
03	Circulating supply		
04	Limited token number		
05	Interest in keeping it staking or masternode		
06	Policy applied to increase its value		
07	Presence on the main exchanges		
		TOTAL	/35
			%

02 – PROJECT

#	Metric	Description + Risk factors	Note (0-5)
01	White Paper quality		
02	Clarity of the proposal		
03	Interest		
04	Market and potential growth		
05	Presence and scope of clients		
06	Competition		
07	Roadmap and respect milestones		
08	MVP		
09	Timing		
10	Realistic fundraising		
		TOTAL	/35
			%

03 – TEAM

#	Metric	Description + Risk factors	Note (0-5)
01	Team size		
02	Previous experience in similar positions		
03	Presence of managerial rather than technical profiles		
04	Experience in fund management		
05	No red flag		
06	Advisors		
		TOTAL	/30
			%

04 – COMPANY

#	Metric	Description + Risk factors	Note (0-5)
01	Existing compagny		
02	Transparency		
03	Partnership and support from VC		
04	Economic Model		
	Income		
	Expenses		
	Risks for business continuity		
	Valuation of the company		
		TOTAL	/20
			%

05 – COMMUNICATION

#	Metric	Description + Risk factors	Note (0-5)
01	Presence on social networks		
	Youtube		
	Telegram		
	Facebook		
	Twitter		
	Discord		
02	Press articles		
03	Regular publishing		
04	Participation in events		
05	Interview		
06	Partnership and support from VC		
07	No unnecessary or excessive hype		
		TOTAL	/30
			%

06 – COMMUNITY

#	Metric	Description + Risk factors	Note (0-5)
01	Size of the community		
	Youtube		
	Telegram		
	Facebook		
	Twitter		
	Discord		
02	Activity		
03	Evolution		
		TOTAL	/15
			%

07 - RISK

#	Metric	Description + Risk factors	Note (0-5)
01	Market risk		
02	Single risk		
03	Risk reduction		
		TOTAL	/15
			%

ROADMAP

DATE	Description	Respect

CONCLUSION

GENERAL OPINION

UPSIDE POTENTIAL

LONG-TERM INVESTMENT

CALENDAR

DATE

EVENT

....

....

....

....

....

....

....

....

....

....

....

....

....

....

....

....

....

....

....

....

....

PROJECT NAME

#

Symbol

CHANGE LOGBOOK	
Date	**Modifications**

BRIEF DESCRIPTION	OVERVIEW	
	Symbol	
	Sector	
	Price	
	ICO Price	
	Market Cap	
	Circulating supply	
	Total Supply	
	Token type (ex :ERC20)	
	Live Product	
	Staking / Masternode	
	Website	

SUMMARY OF THE KEYS POINTS

#	Theme	Description	%
01	Token Economics		
			/35
02	Project		
			/50
03	Team		
			/30
04	Company		
			/20
05	Communication		
			/30
06	Community		
			/15
07	Risk		
			/15
		TOTAL	/195

01 – TOKEN ECONOMICS

#	Metric	Description + Risk factors	Note (0-5)
01	Liquidity Token		
02	Market Cap		
03	Circulating supply		
04	Limited token number		
05	Interest in keeping it staking or masternode		
06	Policy applied to increase its value		
07	Presence on the main exchanges		
		TOTAL	/35
			%

02 – PROJECT

#	Metric	Description + Risk factors	Note (0-5)
01	White Paper quality		
02	Clarity of the proposal		
03	Interest		
04	Market and potential growth		
05	Presence and scope of clients		
06	Competition		
07	Roadmap and respect milestones		
08	MVP		
09	Timing		
10	Realistic fundraising		
		TOTAL	/35
			%

03 – TEAM

#	Metric	Description + Risk factors	Note (0-5)
01	Team size		
02	Previous experience in similar positions		
03	Presence of managerial rather than technical profiles		
04	Experience in fund management		
05	No red flag		
06	Advisors		
		TOTAL	/30
			%

04 – COMPANY

#	Metric	Description + Risk factors	Note (0-5)
01	Existing compagny		
02	Transparency		
03	Partnership and support from VC		
04	Economic Model		
	Income		
	Expenses		
	Risks for business continuity		
	Valuation of the company		
		TOTAL	/20
			%

05 – COMMUNICATION

#	Metric	Description + Risk factors	Note (0-5)
01	Presence on social networks		
	Youtube		
	Telegram		
	Facebook		
	Twitter		
	Discord		
02	Press articles		
03	Regular publishing		
04	Participation in events		
05	Interview		
06	Partnership and support from VC		
07	No unnecessary or excessive hype		
		TOTAL	/30
			%

06 – COMMUNITY

#	Metric	Description + Risk factors	Note (0-5)
01	Size of the community		
	Youtube		
	Telegram		
	Facebook		
	Twitter		
	Discord		
02	Activity		
03	Evolution		
		TOTAL	/15
			%

07 - RISK

#	Metric	Description + Risk factors	Note (0-5)
01	Market risk		
02	Single risk		
03	Risk reduction		
		TOTAL	/15
			%

ROADMAP

DATE	Description	Respect

CONCLUSION

GENERAL OPINION

UPSIDE POTENTIAL

LONG-TERM INVESTMENT

CALENDAR

DATE   **EVENT**

....

....

....

....

....

....

....

....

....

....

....

....

....

....

....

....

....

....

....

....

....

PROJECT NAME

**Symbol**

CHANGE LOGBOOK	
Date	**Modifications**

BRIEF DESCRIPTION

OVERVIEW	
Symbol	
Sector	
Price	
ICO Price	
Market Cap	
Circulating supply	
Total Supply	
Token type (ex :ERC20)	
Live Product	
Staking / Masternode	
Website	

SUMMARY OF THE KEYS POINTS

#	Theme	Description	%
01	Token Economics		
			/35
02	Project		
			/50
03	Team		
			/30
04	Company		
			/20
05	Communication		
			/30
06	Community		
			/15
07	Risk		
			/15
		TOTAL	/195

01 - TOKEN ECONOMICS

#	Metric	Description + Risk factors	Note (0-5)
01	Liquidity Token		
02	Market Cap		
03	Circulating supply		
04	Limited token number		
05	Interest in keeping it staking or masternode		
06	Policy applied to increase its value		
07	Presence on the main exchanges		
		TOTAL	/35
			%

02 – PROJECT

#	Metric	Description + Risk factors	Note (0-5)
01	White Paper quality		
02	Clarity of the proposal		
03	Interest		
04	Market and potential growth		
05	Presence and scope of clients		
06	Competition		
07	Roadmap and respect milestones		
08	MVP		
09	Timing		
10	Realistic fundraising		
		TOTAL	/35
			%

03 – TEAM

#	Metric	Description + Risk factors	Note (0-5)
01	Team size		
02	Previous experience in similar positions		
03	Presence of managerial rather than technical profiles		
04	Experience in fund management		
05	No red flag		
06	Advisors		
		TOTAL	/30
			%

04 – COMPANY

#	Metric	Description + Risk factors	Note (0-5)
01	Existing compagny		
02	Transparency		
03	Partnership and support from VC		
04	Economic Model		
	Income		
	Expenses		
	Risks for business continuity		
	Valuation of the company		
		TOTAL	/20
			%

05 – COMMUNICATION

#	Metric	Description + Risk factors	Note (0-5)
01	Presence on social networks		
	Youtube		
	Telegram		
	Facebook		
	Twitter		
	Discord		
02	Press articles		
03	Regular publishing		
04	Participation in events		
05	Interview		
06	Partnership and support from VC		
07	No unnecessary or excessive hype		
		TOTAL	/30
			%

06 – COMMUNITY

#	Metric	Description + Risk factors	Note (0-5)
01	Size of the community		
	Youtube		
	Telegram		
	Facebook		
	Twitter		
	Discord		
02	Activity		
03	Evolution		
		TOTAL	/15
			%

07 – RISK

#	Metric	Description + Risk factors	Note (0-5)
01	Market risk		
02	Single risk		
03	Risk reduction		
		TOTAL	/15
			%

ROADMAP

DATE	Description	Respect

CONCLUSION

GENERAL OPINION

UPSIDE POTENTIAL

LONG-TERM INVESTMENT

CALENDAR

DATE   **EVENT**

....

....

....

....

....

....

....

....

....

....

....

....

....

....

....

....

....

....

....

....

....

PROJECT NAME

**Symbol**

CHANGE LOGBOOK	
Date	**Modifications**

BRIEF DESCRIPTION

OVERVIEW	
Symbol	
Sector	
Price	
ICO Price	
Market Cap	
Circulating supply	
Total Supply	
Token type (ex :ERC20)	
Live Product	
Staking / Masternode	
Website	

SUMMARY OF THE KEYS POINTS

#	Theme	Description	%
01	Token Economics		/35
02	Project		/50
03	Team		/30
04	Company		/20
05	Communication		/30
06	Community		/15
07	Risk		/15
		TOTAL	/195

01 – TOKEN ECONOMICS

#	Metric	Description + Risk factors	Note (0-5)
01	Liquidity Token		
02	Market Cap		
03	Circulating supply		
04	Limited token number		
05	Interest in keeping it staking or masternode		
06	Policy applied to increase its value		
07	Presence on the main exchanges		
		TOTAL	/35
			%

02 – PROJECT

#	Metric	Description + Risk factors	Note (0-5)
01	White Paper quality		
02	Clarity of the proposal		
03	Interest		
04	Market and potential growth		
05	Presence and scope of clients		
06	Competition		
07	Roadmap and respect milestones		
08	MVP		
09	Timing		
10	Realistic fundraising		
		TOTAL	/35
			%

03 - TEAM

#	Metric	Description + Risk factors	Note (0-5)
01	Team size		
02	Previous experience in similar positions		
03	Presence of managerial rather than technical profiles		
04	Experience in fund management		
05	No red flag		
06	Advisors		
		TOTAL	/30
			%

04 – COMPANY

#	Metric	Description + Risk factors	Note (0-5)
01	Existing compagny		
02	Transparency		
03	Partnership and support from VC		
04	Economic Model		
	Income		
	Expenses		
	Risks for business continuity		
	Valuation of the company		
		TOTAL	/20
			%

05 – COMMUNICATION

#	Metric	Description + Risk factors	Note (0-5)
01	Presence on social networks		
	Youtube		
	Telegram		
	Facebook		
	Twitter		
	Discord		
02	Press articles		
03	Regular publishing		
04	Participation in events		
05	Interview		
06	Partnership and support from VC		
07	No unnecessary or excessive hype		
		TOTAL	/30
			%

06 – COMMUNITY

#	Metric	Description + Risk factors	Note (0-5)
01	Size of the community		
	Youtube		
	Telegram		
	Facebook		
	Twitter		
	Discord		
02	Activity		
03	Evolution		
		TOTAL	/15
			%

07 - RISK

#	Metric	Description + Risk factors	Note (0-5)
01	Market risk		
02	Single risk		
03	Risk reduction		
		TOTAL	/15
			%

ROADMAP

DATE	Description	Respect

CONCLUSION

GENERAL OPINION

UPSIDE POTENTIAL

LONG-TERM INVESTMENT

CALENDAR

DATE	EVENT

PROJECT NAME

# #

Symbol

CHANGE LOGBOOK	
Date	**Modifications**

BRIEF DESCRIPTION

OVERVIEW	
Symbol	
Sector	
Price	
ICO Price	
Market Cap	
Circulating supply	
Total Supply	
Token type (ex :ERC20)	
Live Product	
Staking / Masternode	
Website	

SUMMARY OF THE KEYS POINTS

#	Theme	Description	%
01	Token Economics		/35
02	Project		/50
03	Team		/30
04	Company		/20
05	Communication		/30
06	Community		/15
07	Risk		/15
		TOTAL	/195

01 – TOKEN ECONOMICS

#	Metric	Description + Risk factors	Note (0-5)
01	Liquidity Token		
02	Market Cap		
03	Circulating supply		
04	Limited token number		
05	Interest in keeping it staking or masternode		
06	Policy applied to increase its value		
07	Presence on the main exchanges		
		TOTAL	/35
			%

02 – PROJECT

#	Metric	Description + Risk factors	Note (0-5)
01	White Paper quality		
02	Clarity of the proposal		
03	Interest		
04	Market and potential growth		
05	Presence and scope of clients		
06	Competition		
07	Roadmap and respect milestones		
08	MVP		
09	Timing		
10	Realistic fundraising		
		TOTAL	/35
			%

03 – TEAM

#	Metric	Description + Risk factors	Note (0-5)
01	Team size		
02	Previous experience in similar positions		
03	Presence of managerial rather than technical profiles		
04	Experience in fund management		
05	No red flag		
06	Advisors		
		TOTAL	/30
			%

04 – COMPANY

#	Metric	Description + Risk factors	Note (0-5)
01	Existing compagny		
02	Transparency		
03	Partnership and support from VC		
04	Economic Model		
	Income		
	Expenses		
	Risks for business continuity		
	Valuation of the company		
		TOTAL	/20
			%

05 – COMMUNICATION

#	Metric	Description + Risk factors	Note (0-5)
01	Presence on social networks		
	Youtube		
	Telegram		
	Facebook		
	Twitter		
	Discord		
02	Press articles		
03	Regular publishing		
04	Participation in events		
05	Interview		
06	Partnership and support from VC		
07	No unnecessary or excessive hype		
		TOTAL	/30
			%

06 – COMMUNITY

#	Metric	Description + Risk factors	Note (0-5)
01	Size of the community		
	Youtube		
	Telegram		
	Facebook		
	Twitter		
	Discord		
02	Activity		
03	Evolution		
		TOTAL	/15
			%

07 - RISK

#	Metric	Description + Risk factors	Note (0-5)
01	Market risk		
02	Single risk		
03	Risk reduction		
		TOTAL	/15
			%

ROADMAP

DATE	Description	Respect

CONCLUSION

GENERAL OPINION

UPSIDE POTENTIAL

LONG-TERM INVESTMENT

CALENDAR

DATE	EVENT

NOTES

NOTES

NOTES

NOTES

NOTES